D1259404

NATIONAL
GEOGRAPHIC
KiDS

weird
but
true!

★ CANADA ★

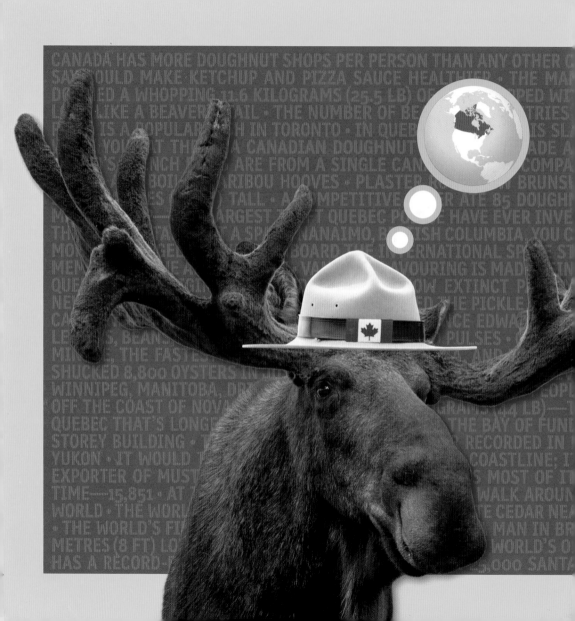

NATIONAL GEOGRAPHIC KiDS

weird but true!

★ CANADA ★

300 outrageous facts about The True North

NATIONAL GEOGRAPHIC
WASHINGTON, D.C.

Dressed in **bathing suits** and **silly costumes,** thousands of people swim 100 metres (328 ft) through

freezing

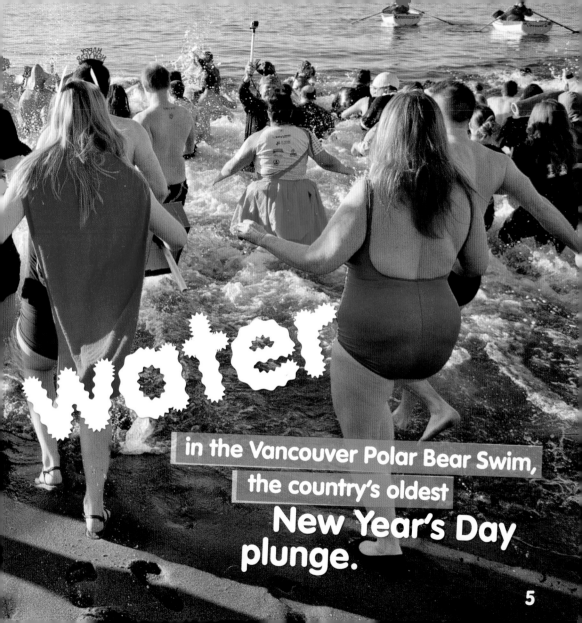

water in the Vancouver Polar Bear Swim, the country's oldest **New Year's Day plunge.**

With more than **350 shipwrecks**  off its coast, Sable Island, Nova Scotia, is known as the **"Graveyard of the Atlantic."**

In Saskatchewan, a hooded sweatshirt is called a

bunny hug.

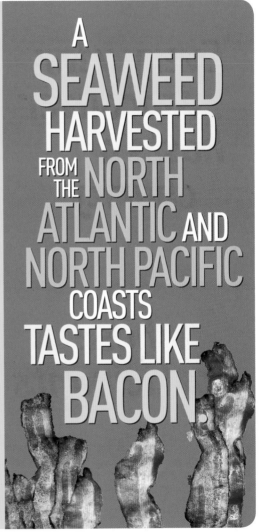

A **SEAWEED HARVESTED** FROM THE **NORTH ATLANTIC** AND **NORTH PACIFIC** COASTS **TASTES LIKE BACON**

Every year, Vancouver hosts a charity BICYCLE RIDE whose participants DRESS IN TWEED.

Montreal's mayor once asked to borrow the

EIFFEL TOWER

from Paris for the 1967 World Expo.

(France said no.)

Residents of
Winnipeg, Manitoba,
**drink more
Slurpees**
per year than
people anywhere else
in the world.

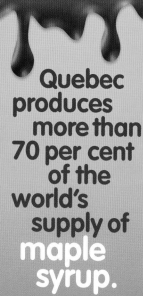

Quebec produces more than 70 per cent of the world's supply of **maple syrup.**

THE FIRST PARKAS WERE MADE BY INUIT WHO SEWED THEM FROM CARIBOU OR SEAL SKIN.

ICE ROAD TRUCKERS

have to closely follow
the speed limit—
sometimes driving only

15 KILOMETRES AN HOUR (9 mph)

—to avoid
cracking the ice.

The Northwest Territories is home to world's

LONGEST ICE ROAD, ICE SO THICK

that it can support a 64-tonne (71-T) truck.

Moose can swim as far as 20 kilometres (12 mi) without stopping.

The Capilano Suspension Bridge in Vancouver can hold up to

96 elephants.

Scientists have **found a crater** in Quebec **that's longer** than the **Grand Canyon.**

A park in Malakwa, British Columbia, is home to more than 350 FAIRY, DRAGON, PIRATE, AND DWARF FIGURINES hidden among 800-YEAR-OLD TREES.

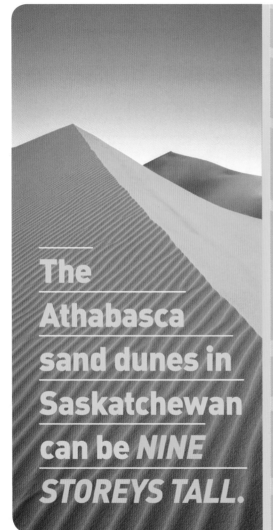

The Athabasca sand dunes in Saskatchewan can be *NINE STOREYS TALL.*

Scientists found **TWO-BILLION-YEAR-OLD WATER,** thought to be the **WORLD'S OLDEST,** in a Canadian mine.

Mother polar bears usually give birth to **twins.**

THE SIGN POST FOREST in Watson Lake, Yukon, has **MORE THAN 77,000 DIRECTION SIGNS** that visitors have left over the years.

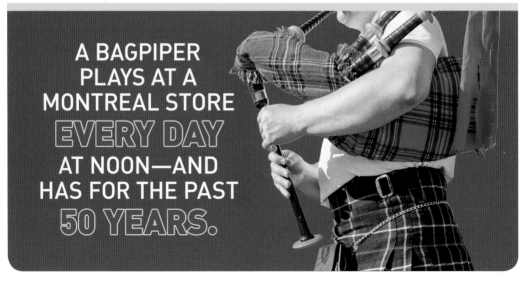

A BAGPIPER PLAYS AT A MONTREAL STORE **EVERY DAY** AT NOON—AND HAS FOR THE PAST **50 YEARS.**

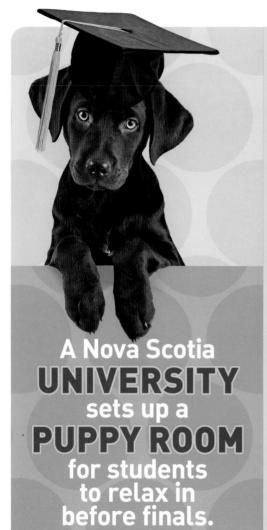

A Nova Scotia
UNIVERSITY
sets up a
PUPPY ROOM
for students
to relax in
before finals.

The town of
**Macklin,
Saskatchewan,**
has a statue of a
**HORSE'S
ANKLE BONE**
that's
9.7 metres (32 ft) **tall.**

Only two
**1911 SILVER
DOLLARS**
were ever made;
today each is
worth more than
**A MILLION
DOLLARS.**

During the annual

Slush Cup

in Banff, Alberta, daredevil competitors race down slopes and **attempt to ski across a slushy swimming pool,** a sport that's also known as "pond skimming."

UNSHINE VILLAGE

Pond skimmers can also win prizes for **best costume** and best **belly flop!**

19

Until 2009, it was against the law to yell, whistle, sing, or "hoot" in Petrolia, Ontario.

At the **CN TOWER IN TORONTO,** you can walk around the outside of the 107th storey— **THE HIGHEST OUTDOOR WALK IN THE WORLD.**

The inspiration for author A. A. Milne's Winnie-the-Pooh was a female black bear cub from Winnipeg, Manitoba.

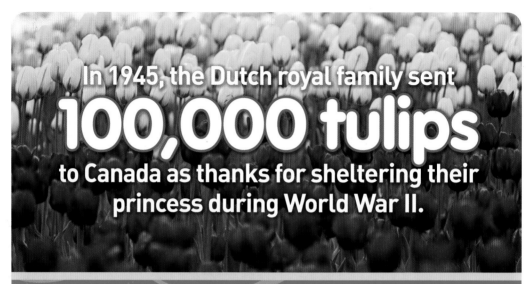

In 1945, the Dutch royal family sent **100,000 tulips** to Canada as thanks for sheltering their princess during World War II.

Vancouver Island HOSTS A RACE in which participants paddle 60 kilometres (36 mi) IN BATHTUBS.

People in Churchill, Manitoba, **leave their cars unlocked** in case passersby need **to escape from a polar bear.**

One Canadian goose can poop about 1.3 kilograms a day. (2.9 lb)

A Canadian doughnut shop once made a doughnut topped with **HOT SAUCE** and **CORN CHIPS.**

Canada lynx will save meals for later by burying them in snow.

Every spring, residents in Victoria, British Columbia, **COUNT HOW MANY FLOWERS** they can find— the record is nearly **26 BILLION.**

Rare **bright blue** lobsters have been caught off the coast of the Atlantic Provinces— the odds of catching one are just

ONE IN TWO MILLION.

The **water** of Manitoba's Little Limestone Lake **changes colour** with the temperature.

Canadian **"Furious Pete"** holds records for the most hamburgers eaten in a minute, the fastest time to eat a bowl of pasta, and the fastest time to eat a hot dog with no hands.

CANS AND PLASTIC BOTTLES WERE BANNED ON PRINCE EDWARD ISLAND UNTIL 2008— BEFORE THEN THEY USED ONLY BOTTLES MADE OF GLASS.

NORTH AMERICA'S **OLDEST AND SMALLEST JAIL** IS IN RODNEY, ONTARIO **—IT'S ONLY ABOUT THE SIZE OF A LIVING ROOM.**

ELEVEN CANADIAN DANCERS WON A RECORD FOR **BREAKDANCING** NONSTOP **FOR 24 DAYS.**

More than two dozen cars are "PARKED" on the seafloor of Halifax Harbour, Nova Scotia, after accidentally being DUMPED by a container ship.

The Old Country Market, in Coombs, British Columbia, has **goats** that graze on its grassy roof.

It was **illegal** until 1995 for margarine companies to colour their product **yellow** so it wouldn't be confused with butter.

Each player on the
**Stanley Cup–winning
hockey team**
gets to spend a day with the trophy—
one player filled it with a
giant ice-cream sundae.

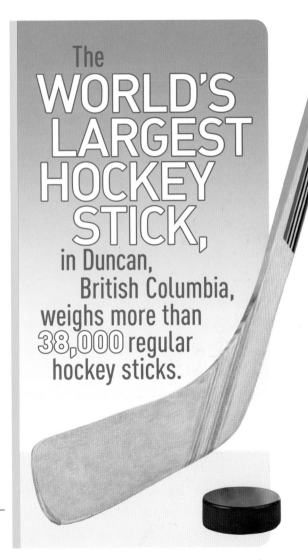

The
WORLD'S LARGEST HOCKEY STICK,
in Duncan,
British Columbia,
weighs more than
38,000 regular
hockey sticks.

In Whistler, British Columbia, brave riders cruise more than **436 METRES** (477 yd) above the ground in **GLASS-FLOORED GONDOLAS** between ski resorts.

Canada's largest
diamond mine
opened in 2003 and
miners have
since extracted

20 TONNES

(22 T, or 100 million carats)

of the
PRECIOUS GEM.

THE FIRST U.S. PATENT **FOR** **PEANUT BUTTER** (IN A CANDY) **WAS GRANTED TO A** CANADIAN.

BEAVERS HAVE **BRIGHT ORANGE** TEETH.

Roughly **1,000 polar bears** spend their winters in Manitoba's Wapusk National Park, one of the **only places in the world** where visitors can see cubs.

The world's **LARGEST LOBSTER,** caught off the coast of Nova Scotia, weighed **20 KILOGRAMS** (44 lb) —that's as heavy as **32 BASKETBALLS!**

The game of **bunnock** involves throwing **horse anklebones** to knock down an opponent's pieces.

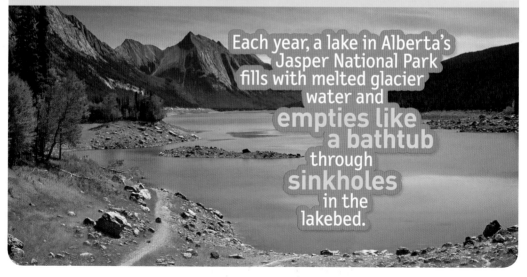

Each year, a lake in Alberta's Jasper National Park fills with melted glacier water and **empties like a bathtub** through **sinkholes** in the lakebed.

Some towns use **BEET JUICE** to melt ice on wintry roads.

The
Pacific water shrew
walks on
water
using tiny bubbles
trapped under its
feet.

COD TONGUE AND PICKLED MOOSE NOSE ARE DELICACIES IN NEWFOUNDLAND.

At a spa in Nanaimo, British Columbia, you can get a **chocolate-sugar foot scrub.**

The Canadian Hockey League 2008 championship trophy **BROKE IN HALF** as it was handed to the winning team.

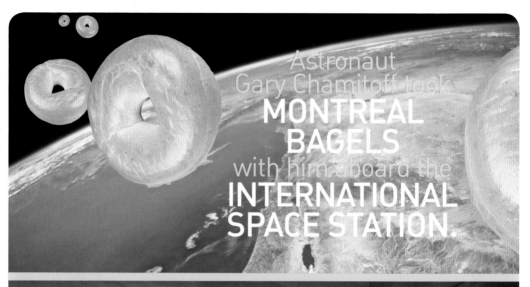

Astronaut
Gary Chamitoff took
**MONTREAL
BAGELS**
with him aboard the
**INTERNATIONAL
SPACE STATION.**

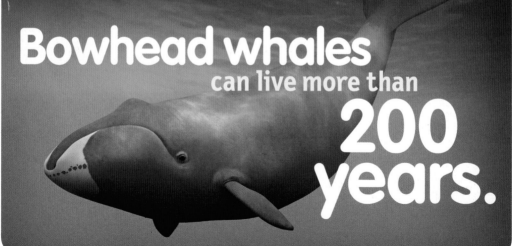

Bowhead whales
can live more than
**200
years.**

Churchill, Manitoba, has heated see-through bubbles you can sit inside to watch the **northern lights.**

Competitors race across a lake seated inside bathtub-size gourds during Nova Scotia's annual **Giant Pumpkin Regatta.**

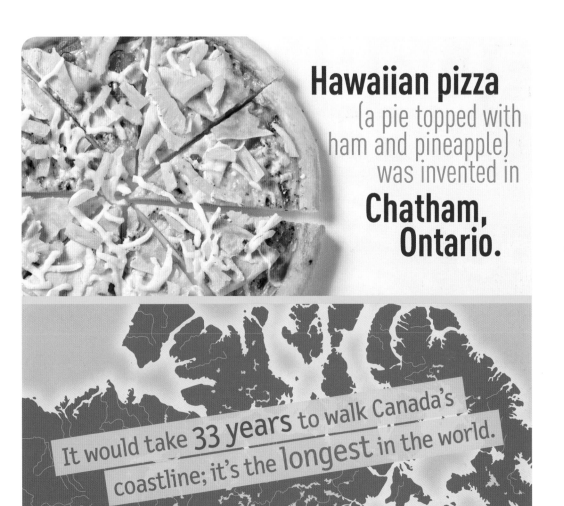

Hawaiian pizza
(a pie topped with ham and pineapple)
was invented in
Chatham, Ontario.

It would take **33 years** to walk Canada's coastline; it's the **longest** in the world.

BUBBLE
SOCCER
PLAYERS compete

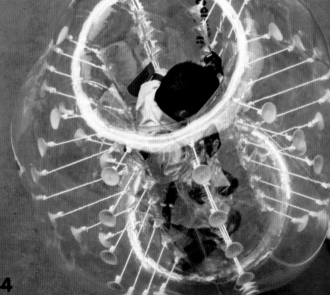

www.bubblesoccer...

while wearing GIANT INFLATABLE SUITS over their clothes.

45

IN 2007, MEMBERS OF THE U.S. GOVERNMENT MISTAKENLY THOUGHT THE 25-CENT CANADIAN POPPY COIN CONTAINED *SPY TECHNOLOGY.*

In **UNDERWATER HOCKEY** (also known as octopush), players wear flippers and snorkel masks and use tiny sticks **TO HIT A PUCK** on the bottom of a pool.

Della Falls in British Columbia is nearly as **TALL** as the CN Tower in Toronto.

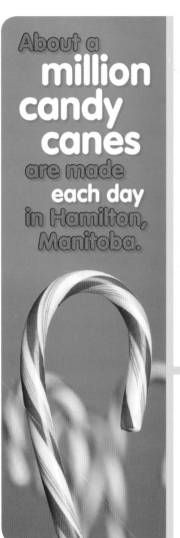

About a **million candy canes** are made each day in Hamilton, Manitoba.

Terry Fox, from British Columbia, **RAN 5,733** (3,562 mi) **KILOMETRES** in 143 days—nearly a marathon every day—using a **PROSTHETIC LEG.**

Pekwachnamay

in Manitoba is the it means "where the wild

Montreal's Festival du Cochon features an event in which **CONTESTANTS CHASE** (and try to catch) a **GREASED PIG.**

CATCH ME IF YOU CAN!

koskwaskwaypinwanik Lake

longest place-name in Canada; trout are caught by fishing with hooks."

Scientists are growing a

PURPLE TOMATO

in Canada that they say could make

KETCHUP AND PIZZA SAUCE

healthier.

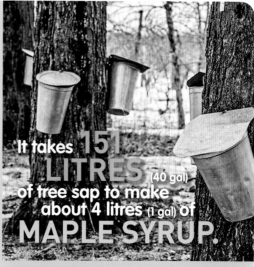

It takes **151 LITRES** (40 gal) of tree sap to make about 4 litres (1 gal) of **MAPLE SYRUP.**

Alberta is considered the **hail capital** of the world— with parts of the province getting more than **40 hailstorms each summer.**

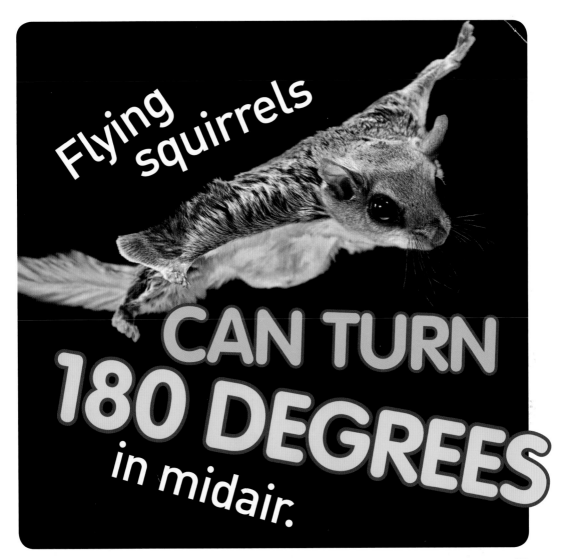

Flying squirrels CAN TURN 180 DEGREES in midair.

Alberta's warm winds, called chinooks, or **SNOW EATERS,** once caused the temperature to rise **40°C** (72°F) in a **SINGLE DAY.**

In Saskatchewan, you can visit the towns of **ELBOW** and **EYEBROW.**

Canada issued passports to **SANTA CLAUS** and **MRS. CLAUS.**

PASSPOR

During **lawnmower races,** *competitors reach speeds of up to* **50 kilometres an hour.** *(31 mph)*

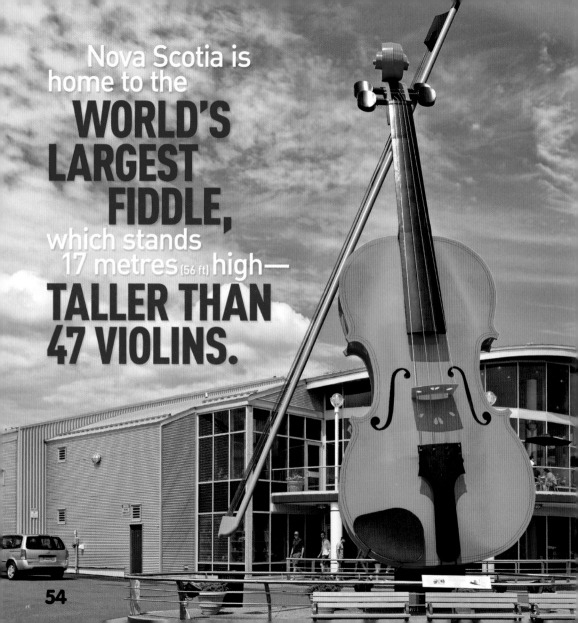

Nova Scotia is home to the **WORLD'S LARGEST FIDDLE,** which stands 17 metres (56 ft) high— **TALLER THAN 47 VIOLINS.**

SUSHI PIZZA
is a popular dish in Toronto.

ON A MUDDY, CRAB-FILLED COURSE IN NOVA SCOTIA'S **BAY OF FUNDY,** RUNNERS RACE AGAINST ONE ANOTHER AND **THE WORLD'S FASTEST INCOMING TIDE.**

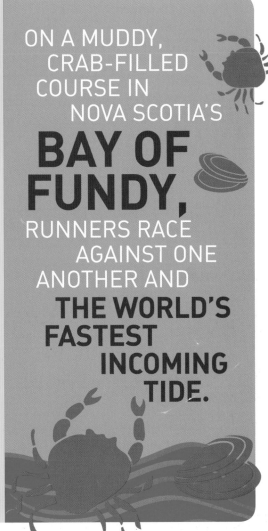

A loud, thumping hum rattles windows in Windsor, Ontario, but *no one knows* where the sound comes from.

A Toronto company invented a

TOY EGG that

HATCHES AN ANIMAL

when you cuddle and pat it for half an hour.

Head to a Vancouver Island gas station to see the world's largest **garden gnome,** made mostly from **trash.**

WORLD FAMOUS GNOME
NANOOSE BAY ESSO

The man who won the 2016 **WORLD POUTINE EATING CHAMPIONSHIP** in Toronto downed a whopping 11.6 kilograms of the dish. [25.5 lb]

In Quebec, "POUTINE" is slang for a "MIX" OR "MESS."

Fresh CHEESE CURDS make a SQUEAKING sound when you eat them.

59

Saskatchewan is the only province in Canada that doesn't follow daylight saving time.

A CANADIAN TOAD

is recognizable by a raised bump called a

BOSS

between its eyes.

When a **wolverine** steps on snow, its paws **spread out** to twice their normal size, like built-in **snowshoes.**

CANADA HAS MORE doughnut shops per person THAN ANY OTHER country.

IT'S A TRADITION IN PARLIAMENT FOR THE PRIME MINISTER TO **DRAG A NEW SPEAKER** OF THE COMMONS **TO HIS OR HER CHAIR.**

Ontario holds the record for **the most snow angels** made at one time—**15,851!**

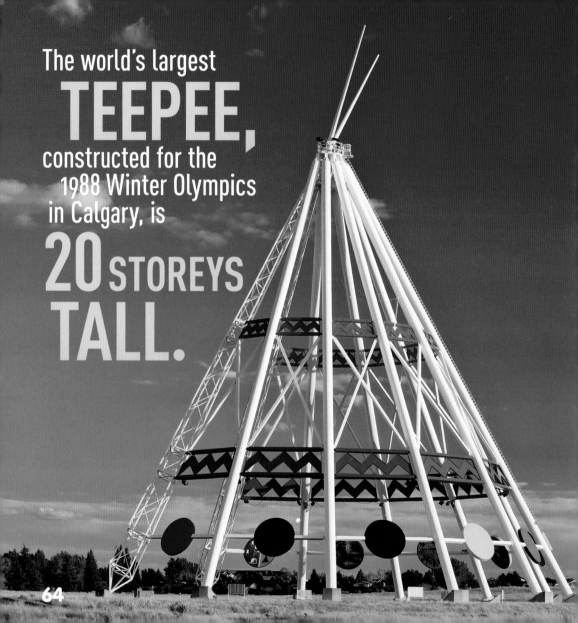

The world's largest
TEEPEE,
constructed for the
1988 Winter Olympics
in Calgary, is
20 STOREYS
TALL.

64

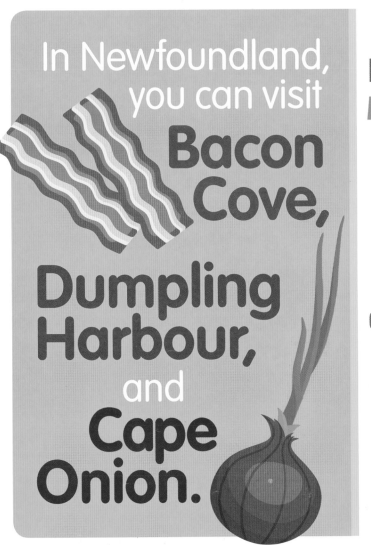

In Newfoundland, you can visit **Bacon Cove, Dumpling Harbour,** and **Cape Onion.**

Two friends in Montreal became **millionaires** after gathering **6,000 facts** and inventing **Trivial Pursuit,** one of the world's most popular board games.

In Alberta, it's considered **BAD LUCK** to pick **BLACKBERRIES** after October 11.

Some hockey fans have tossed **frozen waffles** onto the ice at **TORONTO MAPLE LEAFS GAMES.**

A hotel in Banff National Park is reportedly

HAUNTED BY
AN OLD BELLMAN

whom guests say sometimes opens elevator doors at floors no one has requested.

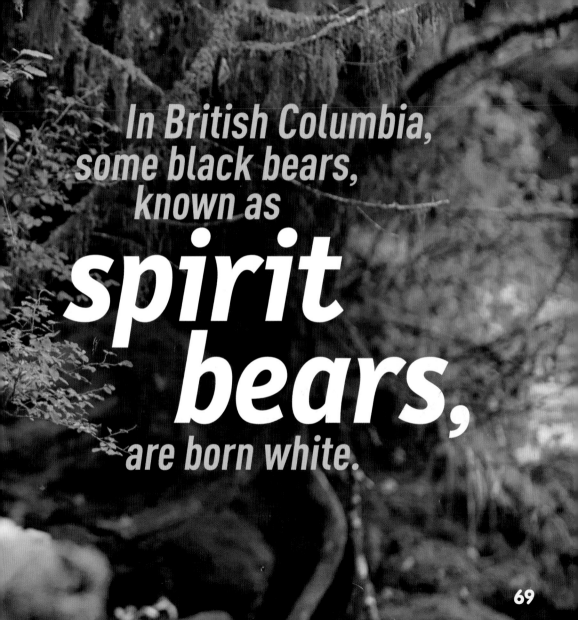

In British Columbia, some black bears, known as **spirit bears,** are born white.

Prime minister **Justin Trudeau** was once a **bungee-jumping coach.**

A CANADIAN CANDY COMPANY WAS THE FIRST TO PUT CHOCOLATES IN A HEART-SHAPED BOX.

A male
BIGHORN SHEEP'S HORNS
can weigh as much as 13 kilograms (30 lb)
—more than the combined weight of
ALL THE BONES IN ITS BODY.

Archaeologists discovered what may be **the oldest footprints** in North America—made **about 13,000 years ago** on the coast of British Columbia.

HELLO, HANDSOME!

Orcas can *recognize themselves in a mirror.*

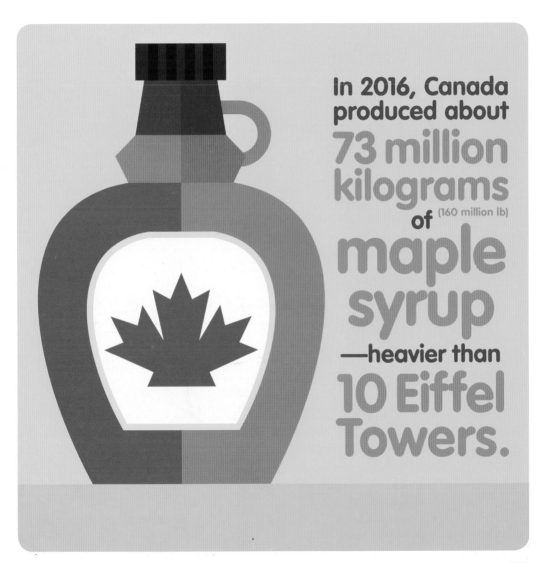

In 2016, Canada produced about **73 million kilograms** (160 million lb) of **maple syrup** —heavier than **10 Eiffel Towers.**

THAT'S WEIRD!

TWELVE PEOPLE

👤👤👤👤👤👤👤👤👤👤👤👤

can fit inside the mouth of the world's largest

DINOSAUR STATUE,

in Alberta.

The town of Mahone Bay, Nova Scotia, is made up of **365 islands.**

During Canadian **CURLING** tournaments, **ONLY THOSE SWEEPS** made with mustard yellow **NYLON BRISTLES** are legal for **PUSHING THE STONE** across the ice.

In Vancouver, there's a statue of **a breaching orca** that looks like it's made of building blocks.

The official phone number for information about Canada is **1-800-O-CANADA.**

Gastown, a neighbourhood in Vancouver, is named after an early settler called **Gassy Jack** who loved to talk.

One-third of the world's **french fries** are from a **single Canadian** food company.

Rocky Mountain air is **SO CLEAN** that one Canadian company **BOTTLES AND SELLS IT.**

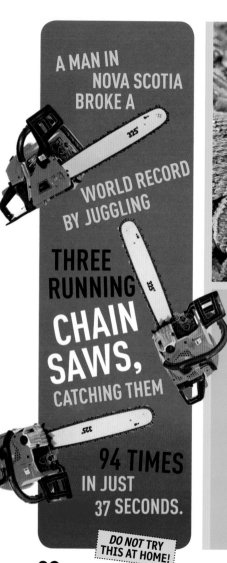

A MAN IN NOVA SCOTIA BROKE A **WORLD RECORD** BY JUGGLING **THREE RUNNING CHAIN SAWS,** CATCHING THEM **94 TIMES** IN JUST **37 SECONDS.**

DO NOT TRY THIS AT HOME!

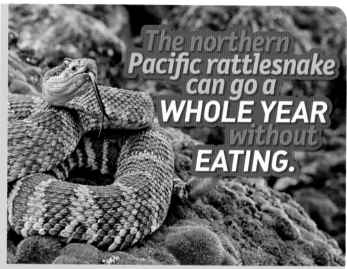

The northern **Pacific rattlesnake** *can go a* **WHOLE YEAR** *without* **EATING.**

The oldest known rock, discovered in Hudson Bay, is

FOUR BILLION YEARS OLD— nearly as old as Earth itself.

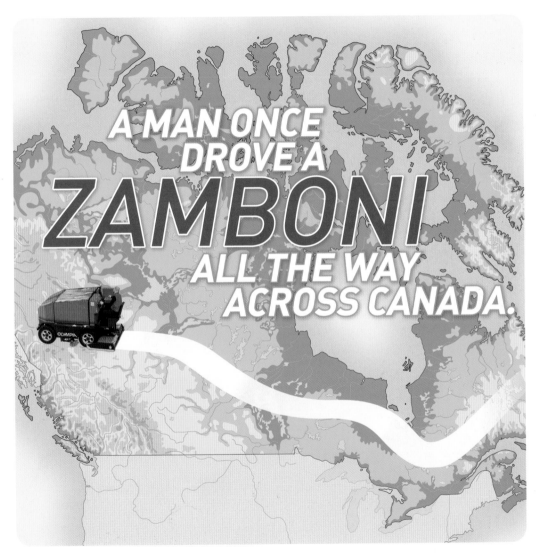

A MAN ONCE DROVE A **ZAMBONI** ALL THE WAY ACROSS CANADA.

The ice in Alberta's Abraham Lake traps **METHANE BUBBLES** that, if released and ignited, can **BURN LIKE A TORCH.**

A **3.5-STOREY-TALL** Ukrainian-style Easter egg in Vegreville, Alberta, turns in the wind like a weather vane.

THE LIMESTONE **WALLS OF** MANITOBA'S LEGISLATIVE BUILDING CONTAIN

500-MILLION-YEAR-OLD INVERTEBRATE FOSSILS.

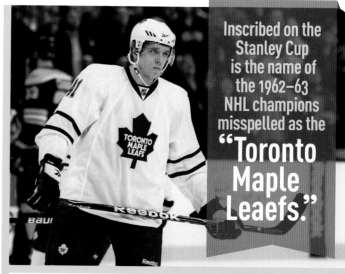

Inscribed on the Stanley Cup is the name of the 1962–63 NHL champions misspelled as the **"Toronto Maple Leaefs."**

Quebec's **Saint-Louis-du-Ha! Ha!** is the only town name in the world with two **exclamation points.**

Canadians **EAT** more than 12 kilograms (26 lb) of **cheese** every year ON AVERAGE.

Wind-driven **ICE YACHTS** glide on runners across frozen lakes, reaching speeds up to **160 KILOMETRES AN HOUR.** (100 mph)

Ice yachts can speed **FIVE TIMES FASTER** than the wind that drives them.

The **WORLD'S LARGEST COCA-COLA CAN** is painted on a water tank in Portage la Prairie, Manitoba.

The Red Paper Clip House

in Kipling, Saskatchewan, got its name from a man who "traded up" a red paper clip for more valuable items 14 times until he ended up with the home.

IT'S ILLEGAL to scare or play a prank on the **QUEEN OF ENGLAND.**

SASKATOON BERRIES, which look like blueberries, are actually members of the **APPLE** family.

Thieves once stole **$18 MILLION** worth of *maple syrup*

—the largest theft Quebec police have ever investigated.

The world's first **million-dollar coin** was minted in Canada—and made of

SOLID GOLD.

A museum in Ottawa held a

DINO IDOL

popularity contest for some of its fossils.

A life-size model of a record-breaking squid caught in 1878 guards Glover's Harbour, Newfoundland—it's **16.7 metres** (55 ft) **long!**

When Northwest Territory residents voted in 1996 for a new province name, **"BOB" was the runner-up.**

Because of a map-drawing mistake in 1793, part of the U.S. state of Minnesota is actually **INSIDE CANADA.**

At an opera house on the U.S.-Canada border, the stage is in Canada while most seats are in the United States.

Candlefish are **so oily** that early pioneers burned them as **candles.**

HALIFAX'S OLD TOWN CLOCK was built by a British military commander who wanted to make sure that his troops would **NEVER BE LATE.**

Saskatchewan's LITTLE LAKE MANITOU —nicknamed "the Dead Sea of Canada"— is **FIVE TIMES SALTIER** than the ocean.

The world's **largest maple leaf,** at more than **51 centimetres** wide, was discovered in British Columbia. (20 in)

The (400-mi) **644-KILOMETRE** Algonquin-to-Adirondack **HIKING TRAIL** was inspired by a migrating **MOOSE NAMED ALICE.**

CANADA'S NATIONAL SUMMER SPORT, *LACROSSE,* STARTED AS A RITUAL AMONG INDIGENOUS TRIBES.

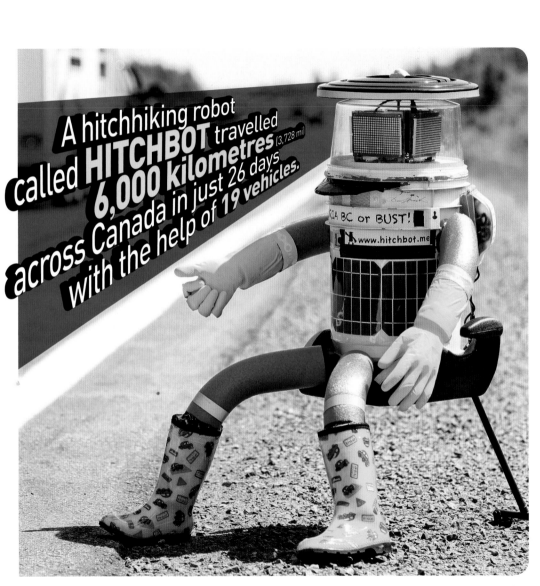

A hitchhiking robot called **HITCHBOT** travelled **6,000 kilometres** [3,728 mil] across Canada in just 26 days with the help of **19 vehicles.**

RIA BC or BUST!
www.hitchbot.me

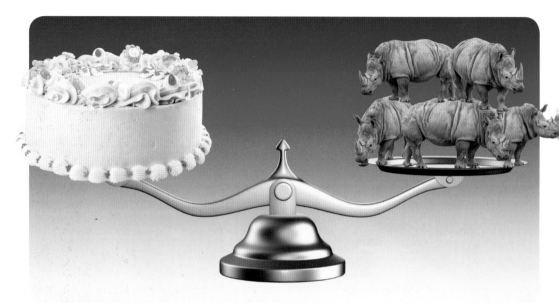

A restaurant in Toronto once made an **ice-cream cake** that weighed as much as **five rhinoceroses.**

Peameal bacon, or back bacon, is called **Canadian bacon** in the United States.

An **OPTICAL ILLUSION** makes cars appear to roll against gravity on **MAGNETIC HILL** in Moncton, New Brunswick.

A group of elk is called a **gang.**

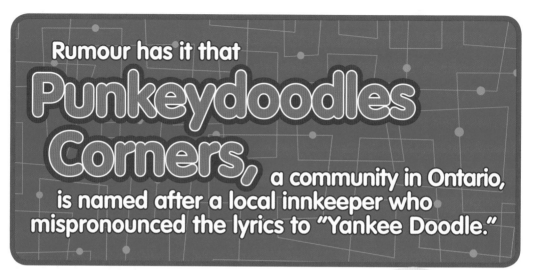

Rumour has it that **Punkeydoodles Corners,** a community in Ontario, is named after a local innkeeper who mispronounced the lyrics to "Yankee Doodle."

WALRUSES CAN *RUN* AS FAST AS *HUMANS.*

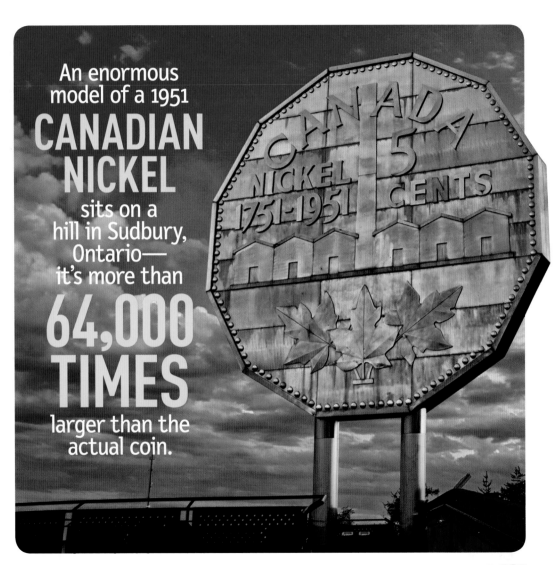

An enormous model of a 1951 **CANADIAN NICKEL** sits on a hill in Sudbury, Ontario—it's more than **64,000 TIMES** larger than the actual coin.

Newfoundland dogs swim with a modified breaststroke.

Saskatchewan is the world's largest exporter of **mustard** —and the United States eats **most of it.**

Without its lakes, Canada would be a **SMALLER COUNTRY** than the United States.

The **giant water bug** (also known as a **"toe biter")** is big enough to eat turtles and snakes.

Mac the Moose
—a statue in Moose Jaw, Saskatchewan—

BROKE HIS JAW IN 2007.

On Christmas Eve, NORAD—a Canadian and U.S. military group—uses **SATELLITES, RADAR, AND JETS** to track the course of Santa's sleigh as he travels around the world.

Before Canada was officially named in the 1700s, *Albionora, Efisga,* and *Hochelaga* were also considered.

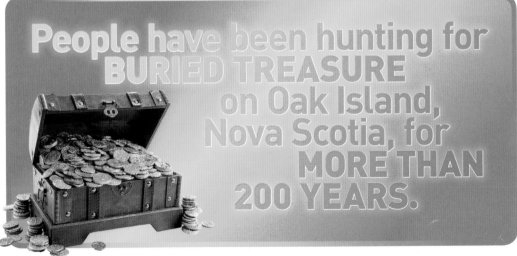

People have been hunting for BURIED TREASURE on Oak Island, Nova Scotia, for MORE THAN 200 YEARS.

OTTERS
USE A LOOSE PATCH OF
ARMPIT SKIN
AS A POCKET TO
HOLD FOOD.

Parking

THE WORLD'S FIRST
UFO
landing pad
IS IN ALBERTA.

Canada's
postal
code for
the
**NORTH
POLE**
is
HOH OHO.

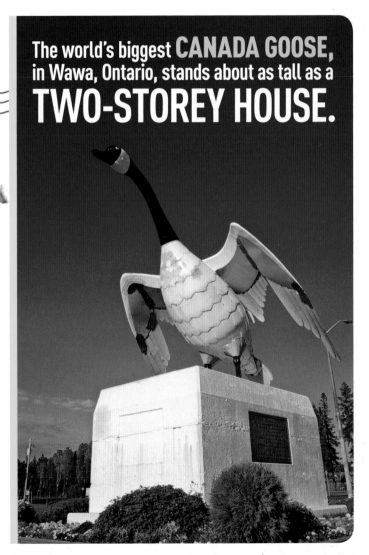

The world's biggest **CANADA GOOSE**, in Wawa, Ontario, stands about as tall as a **TWO-STOREY HOUSE.**

The sand on
Prince Edward
Island beaches
IS RED.

A Vancouver man set a record for doing **THE MOST BACKFLIPS** while riding a **UNICYCLE** on a **TRAMPOLINE: 10!**

A MAN IN BRITISH COLUMBIA HAS THE LONGEST BEARD IN THE WORLD, AT MORE THAN 2.4 METRES (8 FT) LONG.

VIKINGS SETTLED
in Newfoundland more than
1,000 YEARS
ago—about
500 YEARS BEFORE
Christopher Columbus
arrived in the Americas.

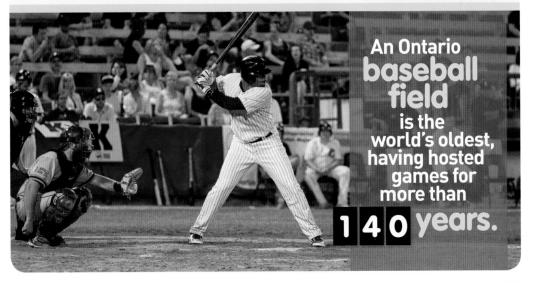

An Ontario
**baseball
field**
is the
world's oldest,
having hosted
games for
more than
1 4 0 years.

Some people believe that **ALIENS** made a grove of gnarled aspen trees, called the **CROOKED BUSH,** that is found on a farm in Hafford, Saskatchewan.

A TORONTO COMPANY MAKES A **HAT** THAT COMES WITH A **BEARD** ATTACHED TO KEEP YOUR FACE WARM.

More than **50 MILLION YEARS AGO,** the **CANADIAN ARCTIC** was home to tortoises, alligators, massive birds, and hippo-like animals.

People say that the mythical Ogopogo of Lake Okanagan, in British Columbia, looks like a 15-metre (50-ft) snake with the head of a horse.

Lentils, beans, peas, and chickpeas are called PULSES.

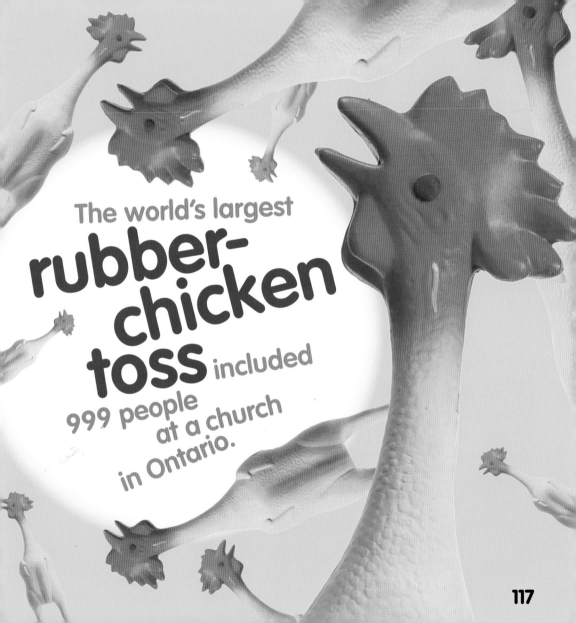

The world's largest **rubber-chicken toss** included 999 people at a church in Ontario.

Winter
temperatures in
Canada can
PLUNGE COLDER
than those on the
surface of Mars.

The world's smallest
snowman was built
by Ontario scientists
using materials
50 times
thinner
than a human hair.

Vancouver's Christmas light maze is powered by more than **85,000 LED BULBS.**

WOLF EYES GLOW IN THE DARK.

British Columbia has a **single-rail roller coaster** that people can ride solo, reaching speeds up to **42 kilometres an hour.** (26 mph)

You can
SURF INDOORS
at a restaurant
in Quebec.

Alberta residents can keep kangaroos as pets.

A team of 10 people once **shucked 8,800 oysters** in just one hour—that's 146 oysters every minute—at a competition on Prince Edward Island.

The world's **largest beaver dam,** in Alberta, is **visible from space.**

125

Alberta's Canadian TRACTOR MUSEUM houses more than 100 old tractors, one of which sits atop a 15-metre (50-ft) working **WEATHER VANE.**

An indoor soccer match in Alberta lasted **30 hours and 10 minutes.**

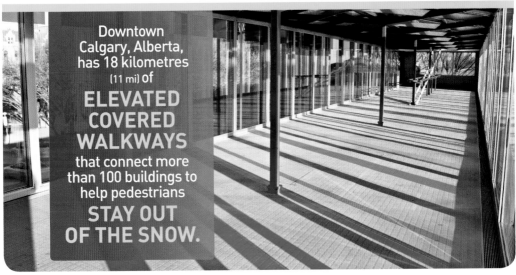

Downtown Calgary, Alberta, has 18 kilometres (11 mi) of **ELEVATED COVERED WALKWAYS** that connect more than 100 buildings to help pedestrians **STAY OUT OF THE SNOW.**

Scientists engineered **canola** —short for "Canadian oil" —from a plant related to broccoli, cabbage, and mustard.

A special "maple leaf tulip"— **a white bloom with red accents** —was created for Canada's 150th anniversary.

FIREFIGHTERS clashed with **CLOWNS** in the streets of Toronto during the **Circus Riot** of 1855.

You can find the world's **TALLEST POTATO STATUE** outside the Canadian Potato Museum in Prince Edward Island.

At the Canadian Potato Museum in Prince Edward Island, you can order **POTATO FUDGE**, a sweet treat made with mashed potatoes.

THE CANADIAN POTATO MUSEUM

"HOME OF WORLD FAMOUS PRINCE EDWARD ISLAND POTATOES"

Welcome

Bonjour

OPEN

A Canadian man has a record-breaking collection of **more than 25,000 Santa Claus** decorations.

WATCH OUT!

Canada geese have **tiny teeth** all around their beaks and **tiny barbs** on the sides of their tongues.

It's **ILLEGAL** in Canada to own comic books with SCENES SHOWING CRIME in them—even when the crime is committed by a **SUPERHERO!**

SPOTTED LAKE
IN BRITISH COLUMBIA APPEARS
POLKA-DOTTED.

Every day, more than 200,000 people travel through Toronto's underground pathways—home to the **WORLD'S LARGEST SUBTERRANEAN SHOPPING COMPLEX.**

After World War II, Canadian engineers built a prototype for a **NEW SECRET WEAPON** for the U.S. Air Force: **A FLYING SAUCER.**

Basketball

was invented in Massachusetts, U.S.A., by a man from Ontario, Canada.

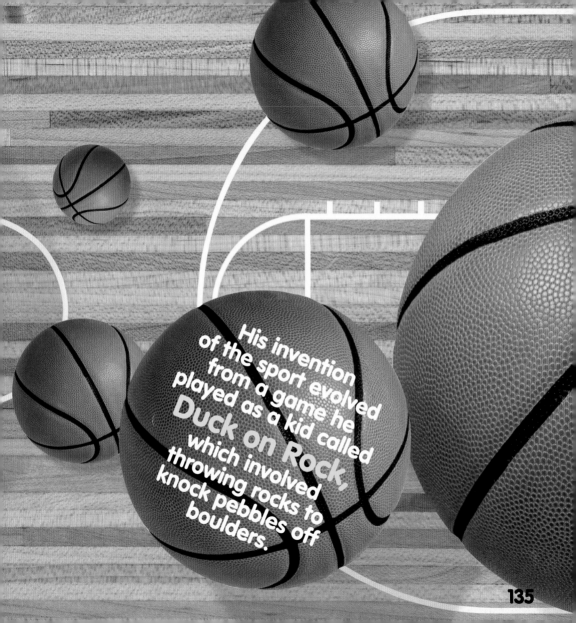

His invention of the sport evolved from a game he played as a kid called **Duck on Rock**, which involved throwing rocks to knock pebbles off boulders.

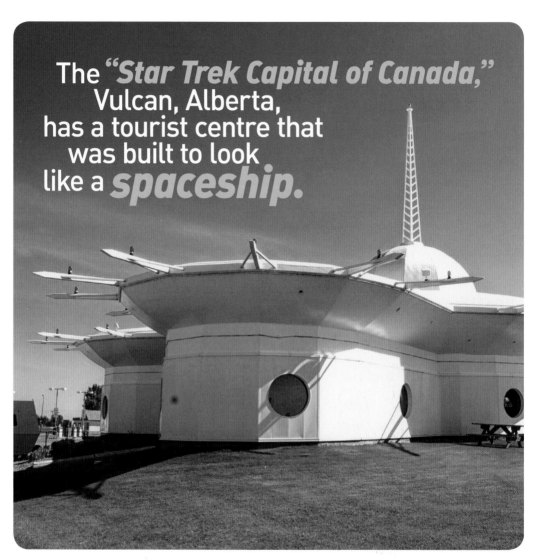

The *"Star Trek Capital of Canada,"* Vulcan, Alberta, has a tourist centre that was built to look like a *spaceship.*

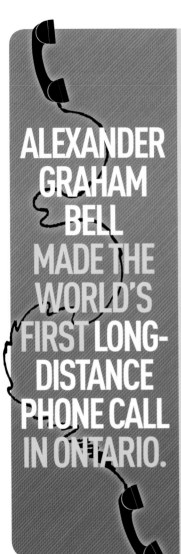

ALEXANDER GRAHAM BELL MADE THE WORLD'S FIRST LONG-DISTANCE PHONE CALL IN ONTARIO.

More than **200,000** **PANCAKES** are served during Alberta's annual Calgary Stampede rodeo.

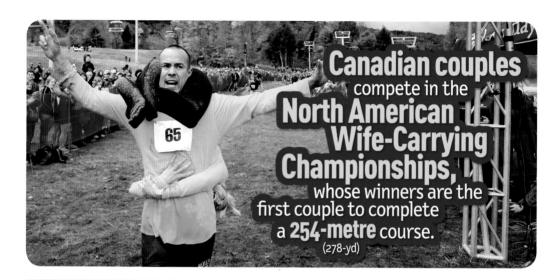

Canadian couples compete in the **North American Wife-Carrying Championships,** whose winners are the first couple to complete a **254-metre** course. (278-yd)

65

A 13-metre (42-ft) model of a **MOSASAUR**

Vanilla flavouring is made using a goo produced from a **beaver's rear end.**

(known as "**THE *T. REX* OF THE SEA**") named **Bruce** is on display in Morden, Manitoba.

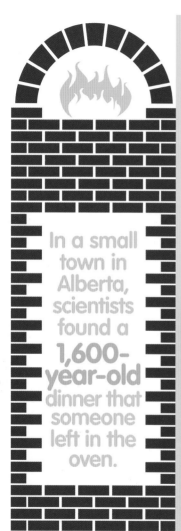

In a small town in Alberta, scientists found a **1,600-year-old** dinner that someone left in the oven.

Tourtière, a **meat pie** *from Quebec, was originally filled with the now extinct* **passenger pigeon.**

People eat their meals in **TOTAL DARKNESS** at a restaurant in Montreal.

Some **puffins** can hold more than **60 fish** in their beak.

Ontario's Camp X was the **first secret-agent training** school in North America.

James Bond was based in part on a **real-life spy** from Winnipeg, Manitoba, named **Sir William Stephenson.**

About 75,000 red-sided garter snakes hibernate underground in Manitoba caverns each winter.

Glendon, Alberta, has the **world's largest** statue of a **pierogi** (a Ukrainian dumpling) on a fork.

Accidentally adding an extra

U

after the *q* in "Iqaluit," the name of Nunavut's capital, changes the meaning from

"MANY FISH"

to

"PEOPLE WITH UNWIPED BOTTOMS."

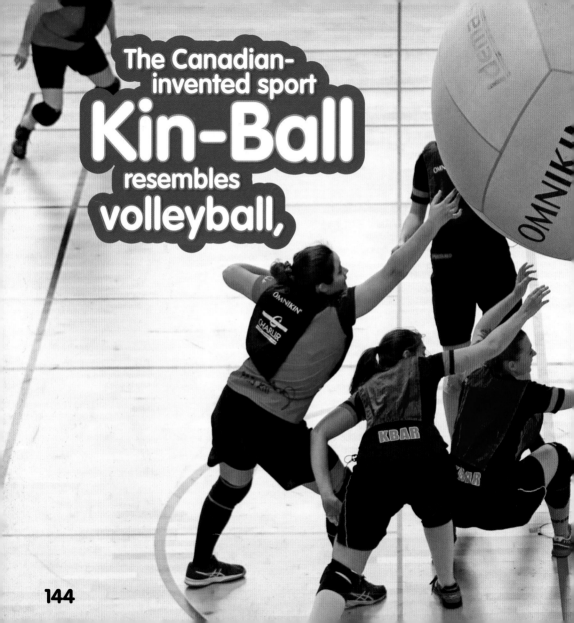

The Canadian-invented sport **Kin-Ball** resembles volleyball,

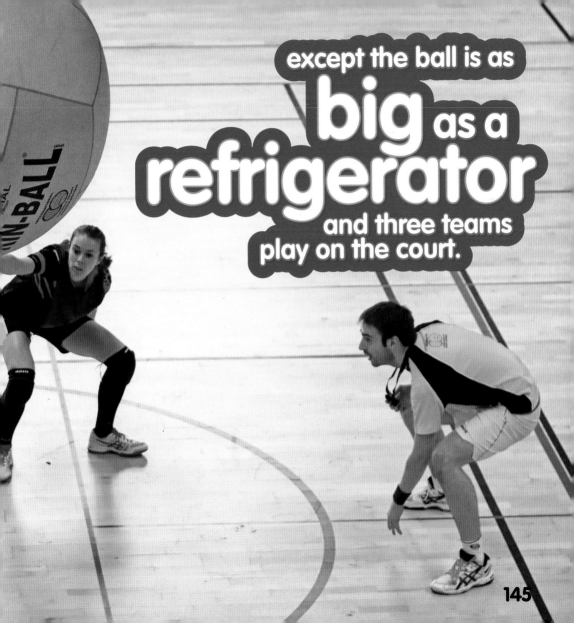

except the ball is as **big** as a **refrigerator** and three teams play on the court.

145

The G suit, invented in Canada, is designed with **SELF-INFLATING BUBBLES** that stop blood from pooling in jet pilots' legs so they don't **BLACK OUT** during fast turns.

The *first person to swim* the 22 kilometres (14 mi) from *Vancouver to Bowen Island* took off her bathing suit and made the trip covered in *nothing but lard.*

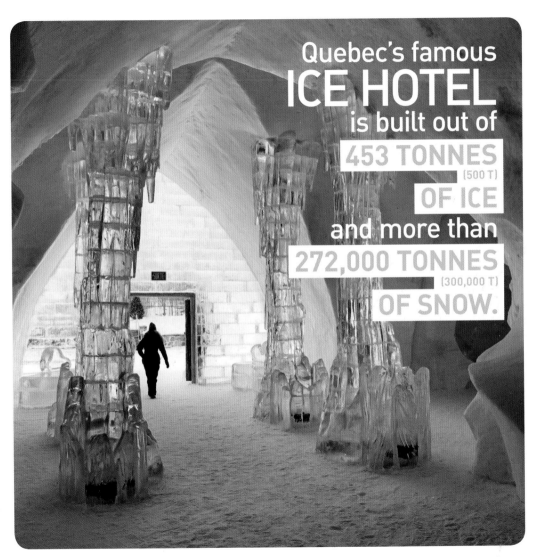

Quebec's famous
ICE HOTEL
is built out of
453 TONNES
(500 T)
OF ICE
and more than
272,000 TONNES
(300,000 T)
OF SNOW.

HOT-SPRING SWIMMERS IN THE YUKON CAN COMPETE IN A HAIR-FREEZING CONTEST

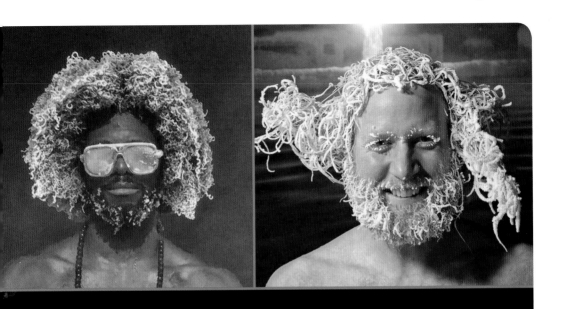

IN WHICH PARTICIPANTS SCULPT THEIR LOCKS INTO **WACKY DESIGNS** IN MINUS 30°C TEMPERATURES.
(-22°F)

If an eagle **loses a feather** on its right wing, it will lose the exact **same feather** on its left wing.

150

In 1860, an Ontario man crossed the Horseshoe Falls section of Niagara on a tightrope WHILE CARRYING A WASHING MACHINE ON HIS BACK.

The first SNOWMOBILES, invented in Canada, were supposed to be named SKI DOGS, but a typo earned them the name SKI-DOOS instead.

You can visit the world's **LARGEST INDOOR LAKE** and **ROLLER COASTER** at the West Edmonton Mall in Alberta.

The mall is **SO BIG** you'd need **72 HOURS** to visit every store.

At Alberta's
Gopher Hole Museum,
stuffed gophers
are posed
in everyday scenarios,
such as having
a picnic at the beach,
**getting their
hair done,**
and pumping gas.

BEFORE CHOOSING THE **MAPLE LEAF** DESIGN, CANADA CONTEMPLATED A FLAG WITH A **BEAVER ON IT.**

After the **national anthem** debuted in 1880, Canadians waited 20 years to hear an English version of **"O Canada,"** which was originally written **in French.**

A Toronto bookstore has a **VENDING MACHINE** that dispenses random old books.

You're
not allowed
*TO PAINT
A WOODEN
LADDER*
in Alberta.

In the Canadian Arctic,
miners discovered the
FOXFIRE DIAMOND
—a golf-ball-size,
187.63-carat gem—
but almost mistakenly
threw it away.
The giant diamond
**GLOWS BLUE IN
THE DARK.**

A Canadian ROBOT named Dextre does repairs to the INTERNATIONAL SPACE STATION.

Special **GREEN INK** invented by a chemist in Canada is used to print **U.S. MONEY** because it's **IMPOSSIBLE** to **COPY** or **ERASE.**

The sun *APPEARED TO TURN BLUE* in 1950 when huge forest fires in British Columbia and Alberta filled the skies with smoke.

CHURCHILL, MANITOBA, HAS A JAIL FOR POLAR BEARS.

Quebec has a special police force, known as the "TONGUE TROOPERS," who make sure that local signs are written properly IN FRENCH.

Vancouver is nicknamed "HOLLYWOOD NORTH" because so many movies are filmed there, even many that are set in the United States.

NATIVE CANADIANS USED TO DINE ON ROAST POLAR BEAR, FRIED WOODCHUCK, AND BOILED CARIBOU HOOVES.

Plaster Rock, New Brunswick, boasts the world's largest sculpture of a **fiddlehead fern,** at seven metres (24 ft) tall.

A HOUSE IN SASKATCHEWAN IS SO AIRTIGHT THAT IT'S POSSIBLE TO KEEP THE WHOLE PLACE WARM WITH A HAIR DRYER.

The **COLDEST TEMPERATURE** ever recorded in North America was **minus 63°C** (-81°F) in Snag, a small village in **THE YUKON.**

The **WORLD'S LARGEST TOTEM POLE,** in Alert Bay, British Columbia,

is about **FIVE TIMES** as tall as a **TELEPHONE POLE.**

Grizzly bears have their own **overpass** to cross the highway in Banff National Park in Alberta.

Beluga whales are sometimes called the canaries of the sea.

In British Columbia's "**cold spa**," you can relax in temperatures of minus 110°C (-166°F) for up to three minutes at a time.

The **first Thanksgiving** in North America was celebrated in **Newfoundland on May 27, 1578,** with a meal of salt beef, biscuits, and peas.

Polar explorers in 1906 claimed to have **discovered a new floating continent**— named Crocker Land —*but it was never seen again.*

Nunavut and parts of Ontario, Manitoba, and Quebec used to be called **Rupert's Land,** after the king of England's nephew.

A **squirrel's heart rate** drops from 300 beats per minute to fewer than **10 beats** per minute when it **hibernates.**

THE UNITED STATES AND CANADA SHARE THE
LONGEST INTERNATIONAL
BORDER IN THE WORLD.

It's illegal to wear a snake in public in Fredericton, New Brunswick.

35% of the music on the radio each week has to be by **CANADIAN ARTISTS.**

There's about **ONE BEAR FOR EVERY TWO PEOPLE** in the Yukon Territory.

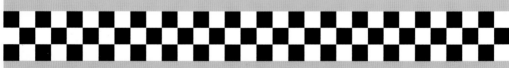

Taxi drivers in Halifax, Nova Scotia, AREN'T ALLOWED TO WEAR T-SHIRTS.

A tombstone in Ontario was inscribed with a crossword-like **CODE** that wasn't decoded until **100 YEARS LATER.**

Every McIntosh apple in the world is descended from a **single tree** discovered in Ontario in 1811.

Canadian-born hockey legend **Gerry Cheevers** drew 150 stitches on his face mask —one for **every time the puck hit him in the face.**

The Bay of Fundy, off Nova Scotia, has the world's **highest tides** —as tall as a **five-storey building.**

Wildlife— **including Sasquatch—** in British Columbia can't be hunted without a license.

A border dispute between **Canada and Maine, U.S.A.,** led to the 1838–39 **Pork and Beans War.**

THE ROYAL CANADIAN NAVY USES **BEAR TRAPS** TO KEEP HELICOPTERS FROM SLIDING OFF SHIP DECKS.

In Souris, Prince Edward Island, you can't **BUILD A SNOWMAN** taller than **75 CENTIMETRES** (30 in) on a corner lot.

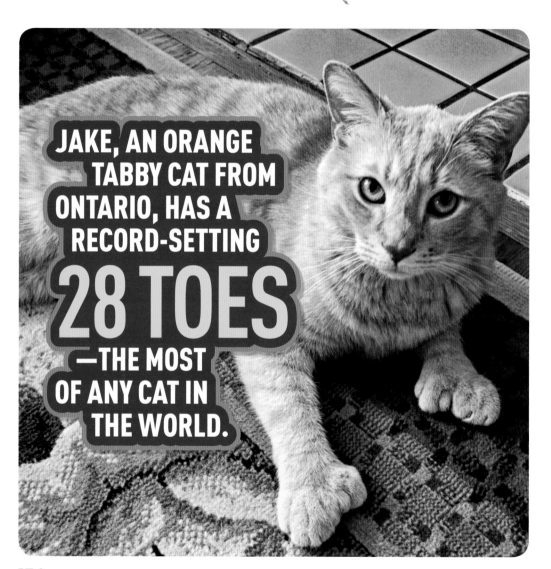

JAKE, AN ORANGE TABBY CAT FROM ONTARIO, HAS A RECORD-SETTING **28 TOES**—THE MOST OF ANY CAT IN THE WORLD.

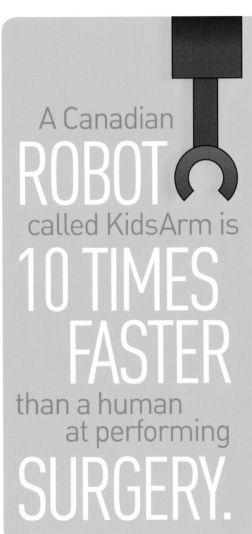

A Canadian ROBOT called KidsArm is 10 TIMES FASTER than a human at performing SURGERY.

A large part of northern Canada has lower gravity than the rest of the planet.

There's a company that makes paper from moose poop and pine needles.

MR. CANOEHEAD is a Canadian superhero who fights criminals with a **METAL CANOE** that's **WELDED** to his head.

At a gym in British Columbia, you can take a **yoga class while bunnies hop** around the room.

NO PET RATS are allowed in Alberta.

AN ONTARIO FARM RAISES **CRICKETS FOR FOOD** —ITS BARN CAN HOLD **100 MILLION CRICKETS** AT A TIME.

THE FARM'S CRICKETS ARE **FREE-RANGE** AND LIVE IN SPECIALLY DESIGNED **"CRICKET CONDOS"** THAT MIMIC THEIR LIVING CONDITIONS IN THE WILD.

179

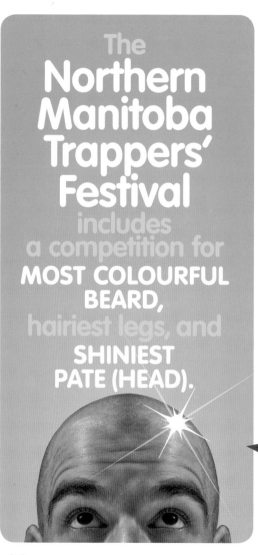

The
Northern Manitoba Trappers' Festival includes a competition for **MOST COLOURFUL BEARD,** hairiest legs, and **SHINIEST PATE (HEAD).**

Musk oxen lived during the ice age.

Battling musk oxen slam their heads together with the same force as a 27-kilometre-an-hour (17-mph) car crash.

A grasshopper **hears** using tiny organs **on its knees.**

A Vancouver fair introduced **THE PICKLE CORN DOG:** a hot dog inside a hollowed-out pickle, breaded and deep-fried.

Reindeers' eyes turn blue in winter.

Newspapers

USED TO BE PRINTED ON **PAPER MADE FROM OLD CLOTHES,** UNTIL A CANADIAN POET FIGURED OUT HOW TO MAKE PAPER FROM WOOD PULP.

The modern **whoopee cushion** was invented in Canada.

The Canadian Eskimo Dog, or Qimmiq, is the **oldest domesticated dog breed** in North America.

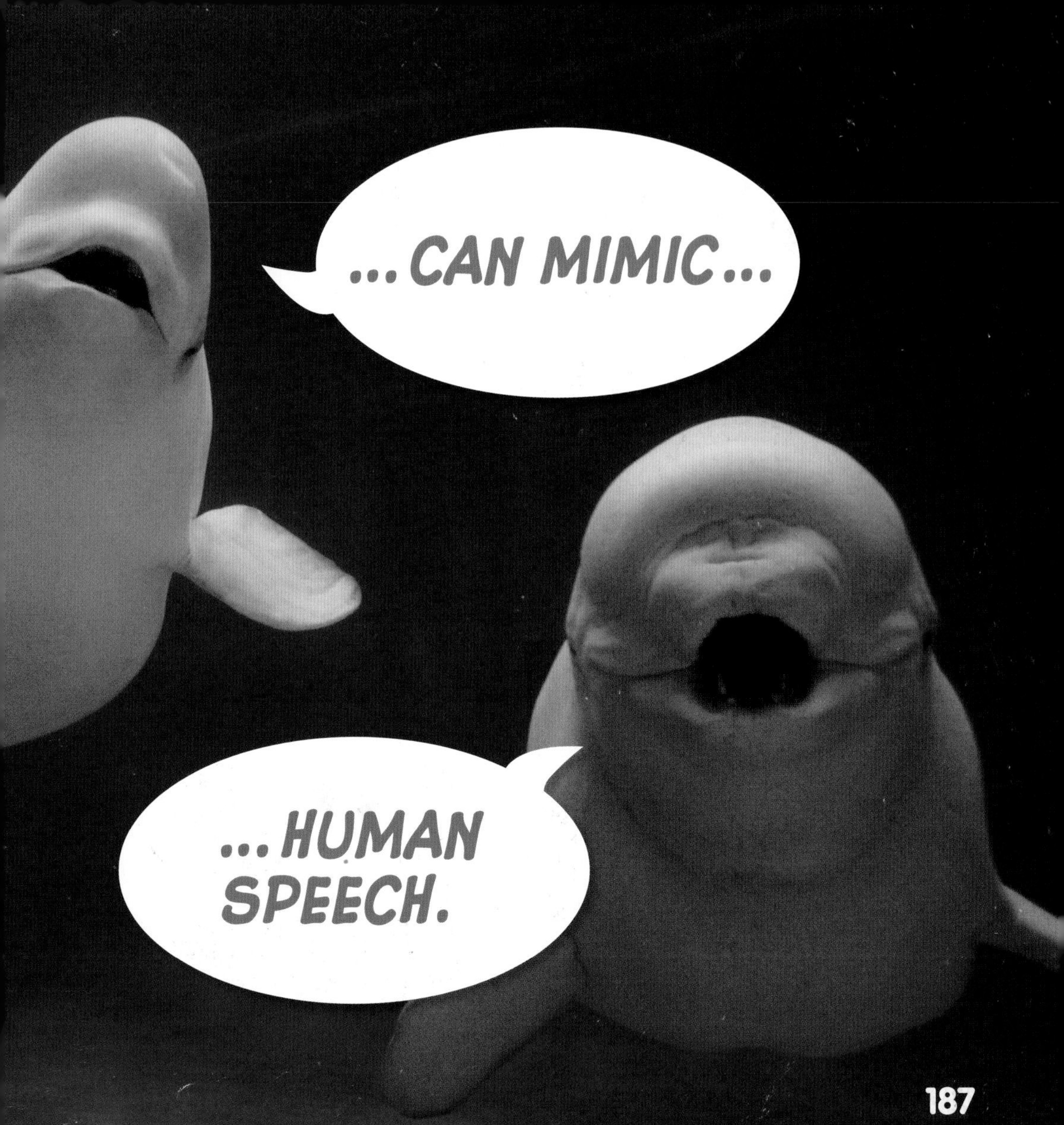
...CAN MIMIC...
...HUMAN SPEECH.

It's **ILLEGAL TO CLIMB TREES** in Oshawa, Ontario.

Canada's name

DATES BACK TO 1535, WHEN FRENCH EXPLORER JACQUES CARTIER MISUNDERSTOOD THE IROQUOIS WORD FOR VILLAGE—

"kanata"

—AND USED IT TO DESCRIBE THE ENTIRE TERRITORY.

It's against the law to CHALLENGE SOMEONE TO— *or to* ACCEPT—

A DUEL.

It took **less than an hour** for a man to pogo-stick up the **1,899 steps** of the CN Tower in Toronto.

CANADIAN ACTRESS

FLORENCE LAWRENCE,

WHO APPEARED IN MORE THAN 200 SILENT FILMS, IS KNOWN AS THE FIRST MOVIE STAR.

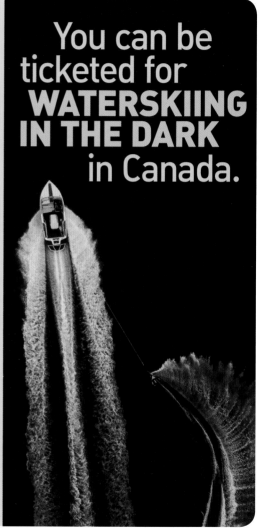

You can be ticketed for **WATERSKIING IN THE DARK** in Canada.

THE LARGEST island-in-a-lake-on-an-island-in-a-lake-on-an-island **IS IN CANADA.**

A former Ottawa **JAIL** is now a hostel you can spend the night in.

You can be a **SORCERER** or **WITCH,** but pretending to be one is **AGAINST THE LAW.**

Police "arrested" a goat for loitering outside a doughnut shop in Saskatchewan, Canada.

192

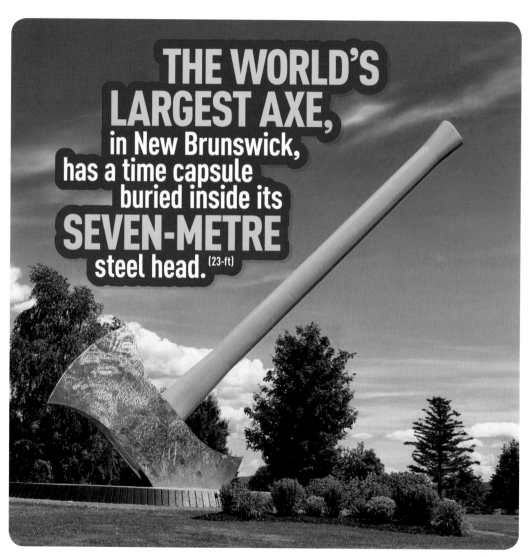

THE WORLD'S LARGEST AXE, in New Brunswick, has a time capsule buried inside its SEVEN-METRE steel head. (23-ft)

FOR **40 YEARS,** PEOPLE WEREN'T ALLOWED TO **SELL STOVES** ON WEDNESDAYS IN VANCOUVER.

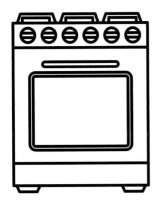

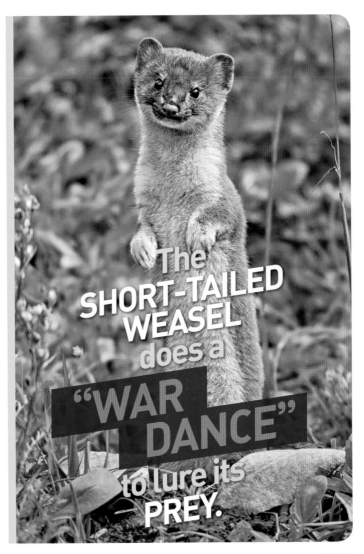

The **SHORT-TAILED WEASEL** does a **"WAR DANCE"** to lure its **PREY.**

Woodpeckers have a **special bone** that wraps around their skull like a seatbelt to **protect their brain.**

The world's **SLOWEST-GROWING TREE** is a white cedar near the Great Lakes that's only grown **10 CENTIMETRES** (4 in) in **155 YEARS.**

Some say
GHOSTS
from the *Titanic* haunt
a seafood restaurant
in Halifax, Nova Scotia.

Moose eat
**almost 10,000
calories a day**
—that's like
eating more than
300 cups of broccoli!

UNDER THEIR FUR, POLAR BEARS HAVE BLACK SKIN.

FACTFINDER

Boldface indicates illustrations.

A

Abraham Lake, Alberta 82, **82–83**
Airtight house, Saskatchewan 160
Alberta
ancient dinner 140
bad luck 66
beaver dams 125, **125**
dinosaur statue 74, **74–75**
forest fires 158
grizzly bears 164, **164**
kangaroos as pets 124, **124**
laws 155, **155**, 177, **177**
museums 126, **126**, 153, **153**
soccer match 127
UFO landing pad 108
weather 50, 52
see also specific locations
Alert Bay, British Columbia 162–163, **162–163**
Algonquin-to-Adirondack Hiking Trail 96, **96**
Aliens **114–115**, 115
Apples 170, **170**
Arctic region 109, 116, 155, **155**, 166, **166**
Aspen trees **114–115**, 115
Athabasca sand dunes, Saskatchewan 14, **14**
Axe, world's largest 194, **194**

B

Bacon 7, 99
Bacon Cove, Newfoundland 65
Bagpipers 16, **16**
Banff, Alberta 18–19, **18–19**
Banff National Park 67, **67**, 164, **164**
Baseball 113, **113**
Basketball 134–135, **134–135**
Bathtub race, Vancouver Island 22, **22**
Bay of Fundy, Nova Scotia 55, 171
Beards 112, **112**, 115, **115**, 180
Bears
black bears 21, **21**, 68, **68–69**
grizzly bears 164, **164**
polar bears 15, **15**, 23, **23**, 35, **35**, 158, 160, **198–199**, 199
traps used by Navy 172
Yukon 168, **168**
Beavers 34, **34**, 57, **57**, 125, **125**, 139, **139**, 154, **154**
Beet juice 37, **37**
Bell, Alexander Graham 137
Beluga whales 165, **165**, 186–187, **186–187**
Bicycling 8
Bighorn sheep 71, **71**
Black bears 21, **21**, 68–69, **68–69**, 69
Blackberries 66, **66**
Book vending machine, Toronto 154, **154**
Border with U.S. 94, 167, 172
Bowen Island 146
Bowhead whales 40, **40**

Breakdancing 28, **28**
British Columbia
forest fires 158
hunting licenses 172
oldest footprints 72
roller coasters 122, **122**
spas 39, 165
spirit bears **68–69**, 69
world's largest maple leaf 96, **96**
world's longest beard 112, **112**
yoga with bunnies 177, **177**
see also specific locations
Bubble soccer 44–45, **44–45**
Bunnock (game) 36
Buried treasure 105, **105**

C

Calgary, Alberta 64, **64**, 127, **127**, 137, **137**
Camp X, Ontario 142
Canada
150th anniversary 128, **128**
border with U.S. 94, 167, 172
flag 154, **154**
name 105, 189
national anthem 154
telephone information 77, **77**
Canada geese 23, **23**, 109, **109**, 130, **130**
Canada lynx 24, **24**
Canadian bacon 99
Canadian Eskimo Dog 185, **185**
Canadian Hockey League 39, **39**
Canadian Potato Museum, Prince Edward Island 129, **129**

Since 1888, the National Geographic Society has funded more than 12,000 research, exploration, and preservation projects around the world. The Society receives funds from National Geographic Partners, LLC, funded in part by your purchase. A portion of the proceeds from this book supports this vital work. To learn more, visit natgeo.com/info.

NATIONAL GEOGRAPHIC and Yellow Border Design are trademarks of the National Geographic Society, used under license.

For more information, visit nationalgeographic.com, call 1-800-647-5463, or write to the following address:

National Geographic Partners
1145 17th Street N.W.
Washington, D.C. 20036-4688 U.S.A.

Visit us online at nationalgeographic.com/books

For librarians and teachers:
ngchildrensbooks.org

More for kids from National Geographic:
natgeokids.com

For information about special discounts for bulk purchases, please contact National Geographic Books Special Sales:
specialsales@natgeo.com

For rights or permissions inquiries, please contact National Geographic Books Subsidiary Rights: bookrights@natgeo.com

Designed by Chad Tomlinson

Trade paperback ISBN: 978-1-4263-3024-7
Reinforced library binding ISBN: 978-1-4263-3025-4

The publisher would like to thank everyone who made this book possible: Rebecca Baines, executive editor; Kate Hale, senior editor; Paige Towler, associate editor; Chelsea Lin and Brittany Moya del Pino, writers; Kathryn Robbins, senior designer; Lori Epstein, photo director; Jennifer E. Berry, photo editor; Sally Abbey, managing editor; Alix Inchausti, production editor; Anne LeongSon and Gus Tello, production assistants.

Printed in China
18/PPS/1

PHOTO CREDITS

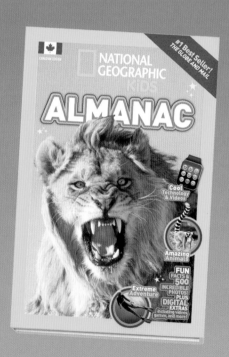

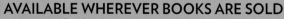